Classical Piano Masterpieces

Piano Sheet Music Book with 65 Pieces of Classical Music for Intermediate Players (+Free Audio)

Christina Levante

Edited by Dragutin Jovičić

Contents

Asturias
Leyenda, Suite Española

Isaac Albéniz (1860 – 1909)

3

Adagio
Concerto in D Minor
BWV 974

Johann Sebastian Bach (1685 – 1750)

Air
Suite No. 3 in D Major
BWV 1068

Johann Sebastian Bach (1685 – 1750)

Badinerie

Suite No. 2 in B Minor

BWV 1067

Johann Sebastian Bach (1685 – 1750)

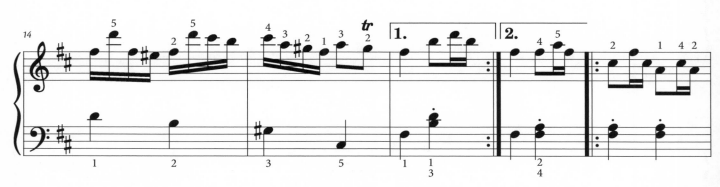

Bourrée
Suite in E Minor
BWV 996

Johann Sebastian Bach (1685 – 1750)

Minuet in C Minor

BWV Anh. 121

Johann Sebastian Bach (1685 – 1750)

Prelude in C Major

BWV 846

Johann Sebastian Bach (1685 – 1750)

Prelude in C Minor

BWV 999

Johann Sebastian Bach (1685 – 1750)

Adagio Cantabile
Sonata Pathétique

Ludwig van Beethoven (1770 – 1827)

Minuet in G Major

WoO 10, No. 2

Ludwig van Beethoven (1770 – 1827)

Moonlight Sonata
Sonata No. 14, 1. Movement
Op. 27, No. 2

Ludwig van Beethoven (1770 – 1827)

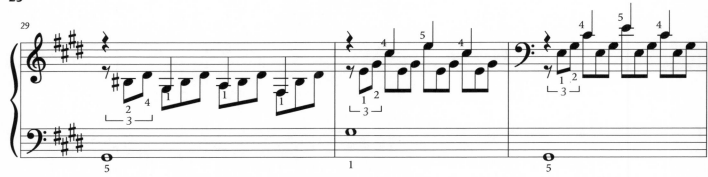

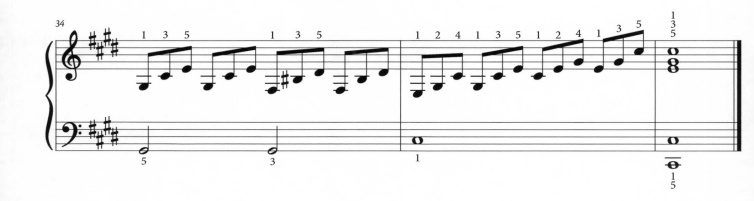

Waltz
In E Flat Major
WoO 84

Ludwig van Beethoven (1770 – 1827)

Minuet
String Quartet in E Major
Op.11 No. 5

Luigi Boccherini (1743 – 1805)

Hungarian Dance No. 1

Johannes Brahms (1833 – 1897)

Hungarian Dance No. 5

Johannes Brahms (1833 – 1897)

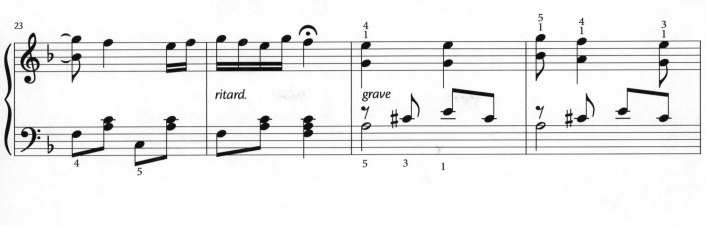

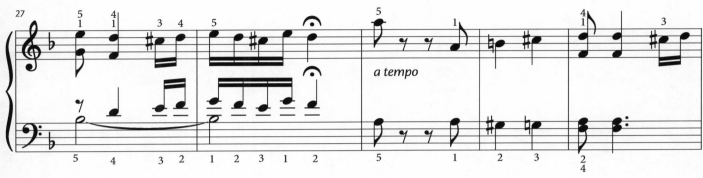

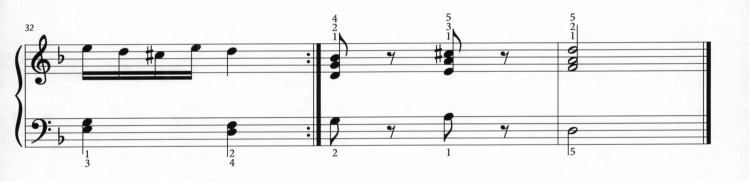

Waltz in A Flat Major

Op. 39, No. 15

Johannes Brahms (1833 – 1897)

Fantaisie-Impromptu

Frédéric Chopin (1810 – 1849)

43

Nocturne

Op. 9, No. 2

Frédéric Chopin (1810 – 1849)

Prelude
in A Major
Op. 28, No. 7

Frédéric Chopin (1810 – 1849)

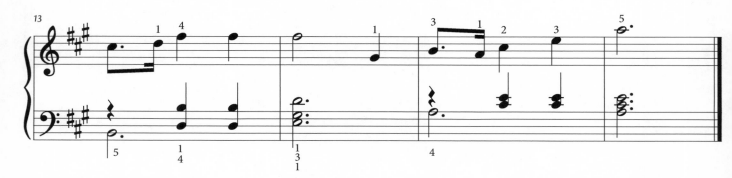

Waltz
in A Minor

Frédéric Chopin (1810 – 1849)

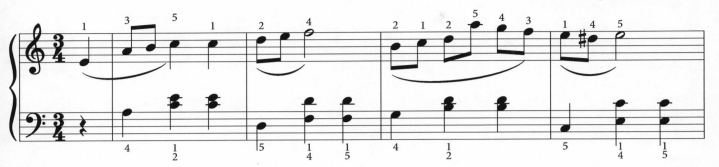

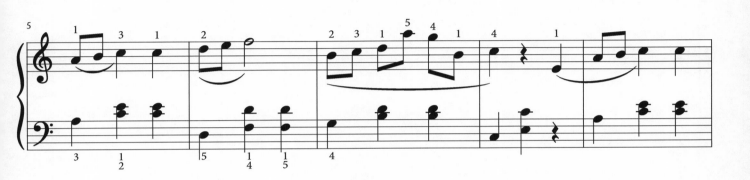

49

Clair de Lune
Suite Bergamasque, 3. Movement

Claude Debussy (1862 – 1918)

The Girl with the Flaxen Hair

La fille aux cheveux de lin

Claude Debussy (1862 – 1918)

Symphony No. 9
The New World
IV. Allegro con Fuoco

Antonín Dvořák (1841 – 1904)

Gavotte
in D Major

François-Joseph Gossec (1734 – 1829)

Oboe Concerto No. 1

Allegro

George Frideric Handel (1685 – 1759)

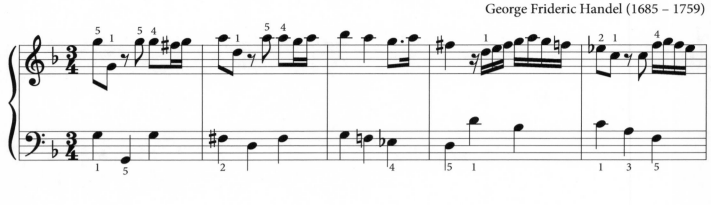

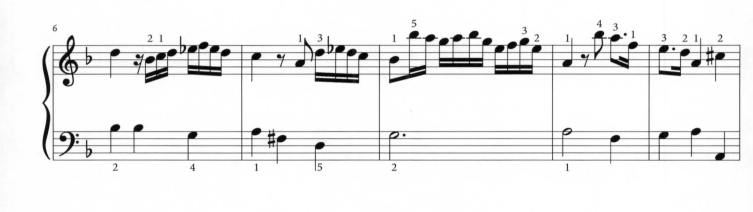

63

Passacaglia

George Frideric Handel (1685 – 1759)
Johan Halvorsen (1864 – 1935)

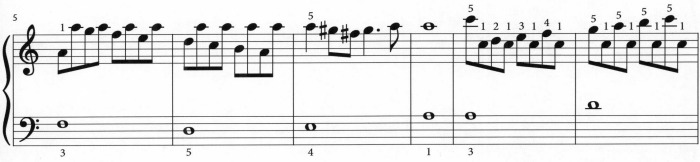

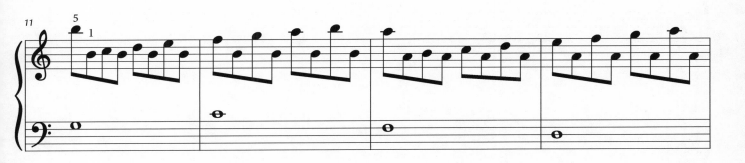

The Entertainer

Scott Joplin (1868 – 1917)

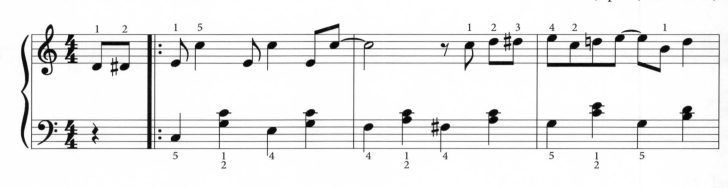

Hungarian Rhapsody No. 2
Friska

Franz Liszt (1811 – 1886)

Liebestraum No. 3

Franz Liszt (1811 – 1886)

Songs Without Words
Lieder ohne Worte
Op. 38, No. 2

Felix Mendelssohn (1809 – 1847)

Sonntagslied

Op. 34, No. 5

Felix Mendelssohn (1809 – 1847)

Violin Concerto
in E Minor
Op. 64

Felix Mendelssohn (1809 – 1847)

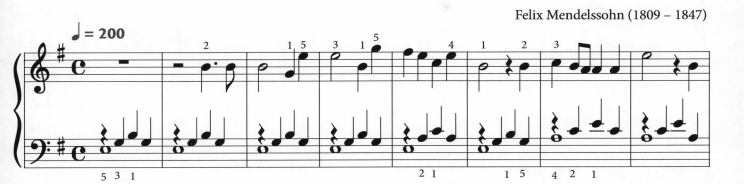

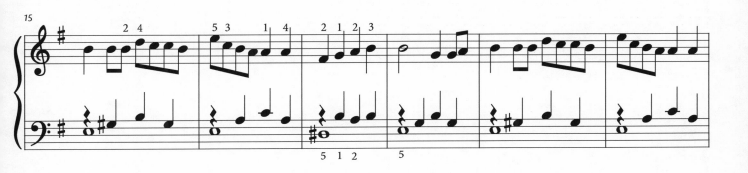

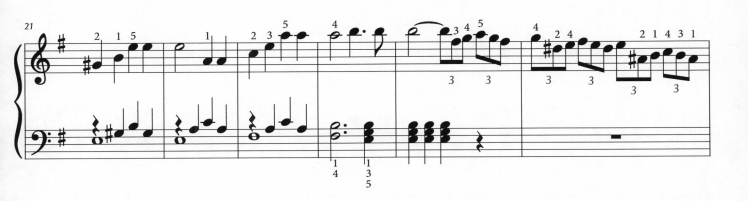

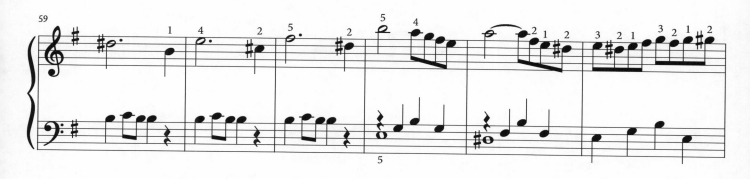

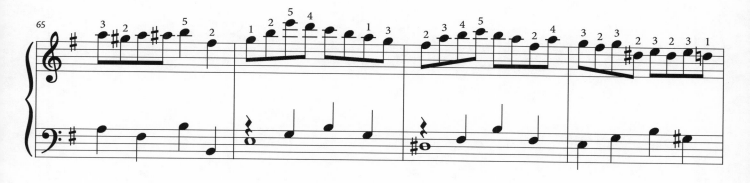

5 Spanish Dances
Op. 12, I. Allegro Brioso (in C Major)

Moritz Moszkowski (1854 – 1925)

Lacrimosa

Wolfgang Amadeus Mozart (1756 – 1791)

Menuet I

Violin Sonata No. 1 in C Major
Op. 1, No. 1, K. 6

Wolfgang Amadeus Mozart (1756 – 1791)

Piano Sonata No. 17

In B Flat Major

K. 570

Wolfgang Amadeus Mozart (1756 – 1791)

93

Symphony No. 40
Great G Minor Symphony

Wolfgang Amadeus Mozart (1756 – 1791)

Turkish March
Turkish Rondo

Wolfgang Amadeus Mozart (1756 – 1791)

Une Larme

A Tear

Modest Mussorgsky (1839 – 1881)

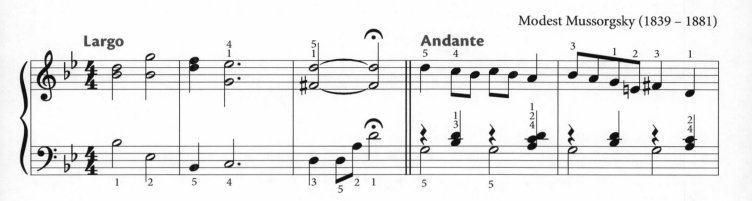

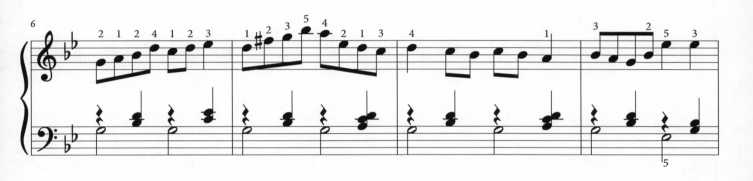

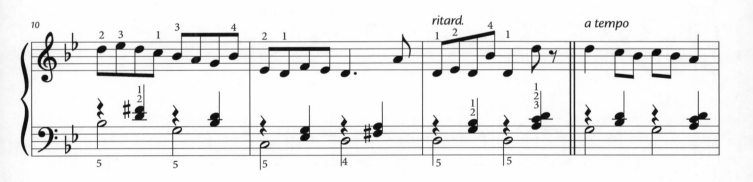

Pictures at an Exhibition

Promenade

Modest Mussorgsky (1839 – 1881)

Caprice No. 24

Niccolò Paganini (1840 – 1782)

Minuet in G Major

Christian Petzold (1677 – 1733)

Montagues and Capulets
Dance of the Knights
Suite No. 2, Romeo and Juliet

Sergei Prokofiev (1891 – 1953)

Rhapsody on a Theme of Paganini
Variation XVIII

Sergei Rachmaninoff (1873 – 1943)

Boléro

Maurice Ravel (1875 – 1937)

Danse Macabre

Camille Saint-Saëns (1835 – 1921)

117

Die Forelle

Franz Schubert (1797 – 1828)

Moment Musical No. 3

Franz Schubert (1797 – 1828)

123

Ständchen
(Serenade)

Franz Schubert (1797 – 1828)

Kind im Einschlummern

Child Falling Asleep

Robert Schumann (1810 – 1856)

© 2023 Sontig Press, Bonn, Germany

Stückchen
A Little Piece, Album für die Jugend
Op. 68

Robert Schumann (1810 – 1856)

The Wild Horseman

Op. 68, No. 8

Robert Schumann (1810 – 1856)

Träumerei
Dreaming, Kinderszenen

Robert Schumann (1810 – 1856)

The Moldau

Bedřich Smetana (1824 – 1884)

Radetzky March

Johann Strauss I (1804 – 1849)

Frühlingsstimmen

Voices of Spring

Johann Strauss II (1825 – 1899)

Mazurka
Op. 39, No. 10

Pyotr Ilyich Tchaikovsky (1840 – 1893)

October
Autumn Song

Pyotr Ilyich Tchaikovsky (1840 – 1893)

147

Piano Concerto No. 1
In B Flat Minor
Op. 23

Pyotr Ilyich Tchaikovsky (1840 – 1893)

Sleeping Beauty Waltz

Pyotr Ilyich Tchaikovsky (1840 – 1893)

Trepak
Russian Dance, The Nutcracker

Pyotr Ilyich Tchaikovsky (1840 – 1893)

Valse Sentimentale

Op. 51, No. 6

Pyotr Ilyich Tchaikovsky (1840 – 1893)

Waltz of the Flowers
The Nutcracker

Pyotr Ilyich Tchaikovsky (1840 – 1893)

La donna è mobile

Rigoletto

Giuseppe Verdi (1813 – 1901)

Autumn

The Four Seasons

Antonio Vivaldi (1678 – 1741)

Free Audio Files

This book also includes access to free audio recordings in mp3 format to help you learn and practice. The pieces were recorded by a professional pianist playing accurately and slowly each song on a piano so you know exactly what it should sound like.

HOW TO DOWNLOAD THE AUDIO FILES?

To download the audio files, go to the following link:

bit.ly/classical-piano-masterpieces

or scan the QR code on the right-hand side.

On the website, please enter your name and your email. Then, click "DOWNLOAD".

Go to the inbox of the email you have just entered. Find the email sent from "Sontig Press" with the subject "Please Confirm Your Subscription". If you cannot find the email, please also check your Spam or Promotions folders.

Once you have confirmed your email by clicking the button "CONFIRM YOUR EMAIL", you will receive a new email with the subject "Here are your audio files!". Clicking the link in the email (or the image) will give you an instant access to the audio recordings of the songs from the book!

You can download each file separately or all files at once (0. Audio files.zip).

Thank you for buying this book. If you are enjoying it, we'd like to ask you to **leave a review for it on Amazon**. It will take just a minute of your precious time.

Also, join our Facebook Group to get more free piano learning material (including free or discounted piano books, when published).

Do you have any questions or remarks about the book? If so, then send us an email at info@sontigpress.com and we'll be happy to help you.

Other Books by the Publisher

Primo Piano. Easy Piano Music for Adults. 55 Timeless Piano Songs for Adult Beginners with Downloadable Audio by Aria Altmann

In this book, you will find 55 musical pieces for (advanced) beginners. The book features well-known world classical pieces, famous English evergreens, and international folk songs.

Little Pianist. Piano Songbook for Kids: Beginner Piano Sheet Music for Children with 55 Songs (+ Free Audio) by Aria Altmann

This book includes 55 very simple and easy songs for absolute beginners. All songs include fingerings and the easiest songs also include key letters. The book features well-known children's songs and nursery rhymes, simplified classical pieces, as well as famous English evergreens and international folk songs.

Christmas Carols for Piano. Beginner Christmas Sheet Music Book for Kids and Adults (+Free Audio) by Christina Levante

In this book, you will find 45 very simple and easy Christmas songs for absolute beginners. All songs include finger placements (numbers) in problem areas and note names (letters). The book features many well-known Christmas carols and holiday songs, as well as some international songs famous in non-English speaking countries.

Made in the USA
Las Vegas, NV
19 July 2024

92605318R00102